THE ARIES PRESS
of Eden, New York

THE ARIES PRESS
of Eden, New York

Richard Kegler

RIT Press
Rochester, New York

RIT Press
90 Lomb Memorial Drive
Rochester, New York 14623-5604
http://ritpress.rit.edu

Book and cover layout by Richard Kegler and Marnie Soom
Printed in the U.S.A.
ISBN 978-1-939125-21-7 (standard edition)
ISBN 978-1-939125-22-4 (deluxe edition)
ISBN 978-1-939125-25-5 (e-book)

Library of Congress Cataloging-in-Publication Data

Kegler, Richard.
  The Aries Press of Eden, New York / Richard Kegler.
    pages cm
  Includes bibliographical references.
  ISBN 978-1-939125-21-7 (standard : alk. paper) – ISBN 978-1-939125-22-4
(deluxe edition : alk. paper) – ISBN 978-1-939125-25-5 (e-book)
1. Aries Press–History. 2. Kellogg, Spencer, Jr., 1876-1944. 3.
Private presses–New York (State)–Eden–History. 4. Fine books–United
States–History–20th century. 5. Arts and crafts movement–United
States–History. I. Title.
  Z232.A69K44 2015
  070.5'930974796–dc23

                                                        2015011840

Contents

Foreword

By Anthony Bannon

As one looks back on the early 20th century, it would seem that there were more people like Kellogg then, than there are now. These were fine men and women of a certain stature and accomplishment about whom, a century later, someone might construct a myth. It is easy in retrospect to read between the lines of their lives and appropriate to build upon and draw lessons from given truths. For why else do we take the measure of such people other than to find our own direction, clear of envy?

Some of their names are legendary. Consider the polymaths Gertrude Stein and Mable Dodge Luhan; Alfred Stieglitz and Edward Steichen; Rabindranath Tagore and Elbert Hubbard. Each one easily lived more than one life, as did Spencer Kellogg, Jr., book maker, gallerist, book seller, photographer, painter, poet, art patron, collector, civic leader, and industrialist.

It is reasonable to assume that Kellogg, a student of the Vedanta, the Hindu monastic philosophy, knew Sir Tagore, the knighted Bengal poet, educator, and philosopher. It is also reasonable to suppose that, based in Buffalo, Kellogg knew fellow Buffalonian Mabel Dodge, keeper of the art and cultural flame in her New York City and Taos salons. It is likely that Kellogg, as a photographer and gallerist of the Photo-Secession, also knew Stieglitz and Steichen, both of whom spent time in Buffalo with colleagues who showed art in Kellogg's gallery. One might even construe that Madame Stein and Kellogg, a frequent traveler in Europe and active in literature and art, traveled the same paths along the Left Bank. And as for Hubbard, he was just down the street in East Aurora, several miles outside of Buffalo.

These heuristic hypotheses do not make the man. More interesting is that he made beautiful pictures, and walked away; he made beautiful books, and walked away; he created communities of inquiry in his book shop and salon; and he created communities around the practice of fine book making—communities built around the process of painting with light or with oil. Wherever he went, people of like minds gathered. That he made art, one way or another, and through it created platforms for discourse, is worthy of our attention as we forge our own way into ideas. Richard Kegler continues the discourse through his fine research and rhetoric, taking us the first several miles. The rest will be up to the reader.

Anthony Bannon, Ph.D., is director of the Burchfield Penney Art Center at SUNY Buffalo State College and a research professor at the College. His book, *The Photo-Pictorialists of Buffalo* (1981), recounts Kellogg's contributions to photography as a member of the Buffalo Camera Club and colleague in the American Photo-Secessionist movement. He served as director of George Eastman House International Museum of Photography and Film from 1996 to 2012.

Introduction

William Morris (1834–1896) is often cited as the single most influential figure in the Arts and Crafts movement, which emerged during the late Victorian era. His various areas of interest, expertise, and influence included architecture, textiles, stained glass, wallpapers, and fine book printing. After listening to a talk by English printer Emery Walker in 1888, Morris was inspired to start his own press and create his own typefaces.[1] Morris's Kelmscott Press produced exceptional handmade books that set the standard for fine book printing and are still held as the high-water mark for the private-press movement it helped to launch. Other English presses such as the Doves (an infamous partnership between Emery Walker and T.J. Cobden-Sanderson[2]), Ashendene, Vale, and Essex are all highly regarded and known for adhering to the ideals of Morris. The private-press movement also elevated the art of the book far above the inferior mass-produced books that were typical of the quantity-over-quality ethos of the Industrial Revolution.

Morris's influence continued to spread as private presses around the world soon followed the Kelmscott example. In the United States, the Roycroft Press, founded by industrialist-turned-aesthete Elbert Hubbard, took the Kelmscott Press as founding inspiration, though it ultimately printed millions of books. Other presses in the United States and elsewhere took inspiration from the fine editions of the private-press world and eventually cross-pollinated with commercial interests to elevate the standards of trade books.

Rogers, Goudy, Dwiggins, Updike, and Cleland are names well known in all surveys of American book design of the early 20th century. There are others of course, but a casual look through the annual American Institute of Graphic Arts's (AIGA) list of the 50 best-designed books will find these names with some consistency. Leading off the list in 1926, (which was organized alphabetically by publisher), was a book designed by the relatively unknown name Spencer Kellogg, Jr. The book, *The Ghost Ship* by Richard Middleton, was also the first book printed at the Aries Press of Eden, New York. The Aries Press was a very modest operation with two key figures. It was probably similar to many other earnest and dedicated private presses throughout America and Europe. Aries produced only a handful of books, and editions numbered no more than 300 for any given title. What was exceptional were the Press's direct connections to William Morris, Rockwell Kent, Bruce Rogers, Frederic Goudy, and a host of other book-arts luminaries of the early 20th century.

The Aries Press was the brainchild of Spencer Kellogg Jr., a wealthy businessman, like Elbert Hubbard, who decided to turn all of his attention to aesthetic concerns and leave the family business to

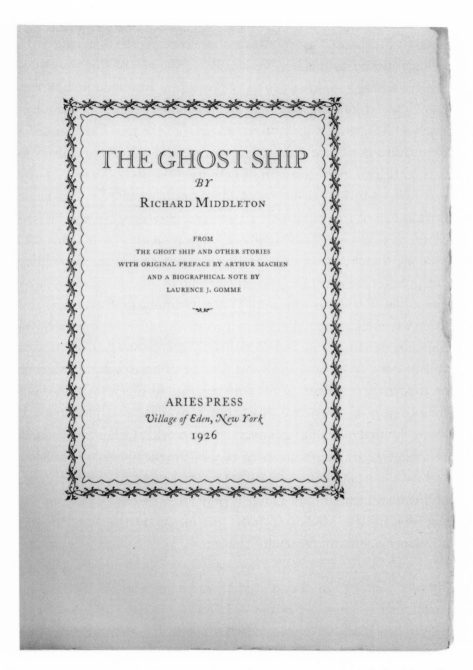

THE GHOST SHIP
BY
RICHARD MIDDLETON

FROM
THE GHOST SHIP AND OTHER STORIES
WITH ORIGINAL PREFACE BY ARTHUR MACHEN
AND A BIOGRAPHICAL NOTE BY
LAURENCE J. GOMME

ARIES PRESS
Village of Eden, New York
1926

Title page from the first official book printed by Aries Press, entitled *The Ghost Ship*.

his two brothers. Born in Amsterdam, New York, April 10, 1876, Kellogg moved to Buffalo, New York, at the age of three with his family, where his father started a linseed oil business. Buffalo was chosen as an ideal location for this business considering the city's strategic location as the western terminus of the Erie Canal and the gateway to the Great Lakes. The storage and shipping facilities in Buffalo were a non-stop hub of activity. The development of the grain elevator as a utilitarian and engineering marvel also made Buffalo one of the wealthiest cities per capita in all of the United States at that time. Structurally, the grain elevator was influential to modern architecture as it employed a new technique in building with reinforced concrete, and was devoid of any unnecessary orna-mentation. European architects Walter Gropius, Le Corbusier, and Erich Mendelsohn extolled the virtues of the ultimate "form follows function" structures in Buffalo that later influenced Bauhaus design and modern architecture in general[3]. The grain elevators' influence on modern architecture was of no concern to the practical side of the business, as Spencer Kellogg and Sons went on to become the largest linseed oil milling company in the world[4]. Other by-products of commerce and concentrations of wealth contributed to Buffalo's architectural landscape as well, through commissions from Louis Sullivan and from Frank Lloyd Wright. It is fortunate that, in the tradition of the Medici of Italy, patronage by the wealthy can develop a significant legacy for the arts.

Spencer Kellogg, Jr. was an active participant in the Buffalo art world, first as a member of the Buffalo Camera Club and the Photo-Pictorialists from 1905 through 1925.[5] The Buffalo Photo-Pictorialists were turn-of-the-century photographers whose poetic style of land-scape photography took the relatively young medium of photography

Portrait of Spencer Kellogg Jr. by Clara E. Sipprell. Image courtesy of
Special Collections Research Center, Syracuse University Library.

into dreamlike territory, and away from literal documentation and representation. The Buffalo School of Photography was internationally recognized and friendly with Alfred Stieglitz's Photo-Secessionist movement. From 1913 to 1914, Kellogg hosted exhibitions in his own home, showcasing prominent Photo-Pictorialists and Secessionists, though rarely exhibiting his own work. Kellogg also served as a director of the Buffalo Fine Arts Academy (the Albright Art Gallery, now known as the Albright-Knox Art Gallery) from 1916 to 1919 and again from 1924 to 1927. As a collector, he lent works to exhibitions and eventually donated much of his book collection to the Albright Art Gallery library, which later donated many of the books to the University at Buffalo Library.

He was a member of several clubs, including the Grolier and Salmagundi clubs in New York City. By 1922, Kellogg had officially retired as vice president of Spencer Kellogg and Sons. His father's death that year helped him decide "to do exactly as he pleased"[6] and plan his expansion from the newly opened Aries Book Shop towards his private press. Kellogg's love of art and travel was well known, and his likely patrons were friends and associates of similar means and interests. One such peer was Darwin D. Martin, an executive with the Larkin Soap Company of Buffalo.[7] Martin was a great patron and friend of Frank Lloyd Wright at a time when Wright was financially troubled. In two letters to Wright, a frustrated Martin suggests Kellogg as a possible solution to Wright's debt burden to Martin:

> *Apr 21 1919*
> *I hear that Spencer Kellogg, Jr. of Buffalo, second generation millionaire, has in California become an enthusiast on [sic] Japanese prints...I am told that to realize on the*

security in the form of Prints which I hold from you, I must do something like Auctioning them on the Cook County Court House steps. Can we not arrange to do away with that formality, perhaps to your advantage?...I rather think you could separate Mr. Kellogg from more money than I could, if he is sellable. You have a way with you.[8]

Wright did not likely contact Kellogg, as Martin tries again three years later:

Aug 28, 1922
...Were I acidly to tell you that your investment in objets d'art is of funds withheld from a creditor, you would at once recognize that I have not grown with you. I think it is true that in this case the leopard has not changed his spots. Of course, you have felt that you could do better for your creditor by such investment than he could have himself—if you analyzed it to yourself at all.

The possible patron for Japanese prints, whose name I gave you a year or two ago is Spencer Kellogg, Jr. proprietor Aries Book Shop, 116 Delaware Avenue, Buffalo, whom I have no doubt you can interview at any time you are passing through Buffalo.[9]

The Aries Book Shop

Kellogg's love of books manifested itself in his Aries Book Shop and Cronies' Book Club, both located in downtown Buffalo, adjacent to the offices of Spencer Kellogg and Sons, Inc. The Aries Book Shop served as a gathering place for fellow bibliophiles and was the incubator for the Aries Press. Through personal correspondence and published newspaper accounts,[10] it appears that the Aries Book Shop never made any money, nor did Kellogg expect it to. In 1921, when Kellogg opened his shop, he enlisted the assistance of Laurence Gomme of the Neighborhood Bookshop in New York. Laurence Gomme contributed a biographical note to the first Aries book, *The Ghost Ship*, in 1925. Gomme previously ran The Little Book-Shop Around the Corner (Little Book Shop), which was started by publisher Mitchell Kennerley in 1907. The Little Book Shop was the type of venture that Kellogg aspired to open in Buffalo. The store would be a comfortable retreat into a world of books, where noted speakers could hold informal talks, and where small exhibitions could be displayed, a shop where the clientele was as interesting as the books. Gomme recalled one particular visitor:

> I remember among our very first visitors was a rotund stooping figure requesting to see Mr. Kennerley. After giving his name I led him into the inner office. The following day he returned. To my dismay I had forgotten his name! Seeing my hesitancy, he replied with disconcerting truth, "Same as yesterday—Goudy." This was the strange beginning of a long and valued friendship. It was my introduction to the art of typography. He was designing a type for the handsomely planned edition of The Door in the Wall for Mitchell Kennerley, later named for his patron, "Kennerley."[11]

Frederic W. Goudy was the preeminent type designer of his day, and considered by many to be one of the most influential type designers ever. He was also a book designer and proprietor of the Village Press. With a move of the Village Press to Manhattan in 1906, and partly due to his association with Kennerley, Goudy was able to keep busy with type and book design commissions. In early 1908, a fire destroyed the Manhattan office of the Village Press. Goudy soon set up an office in a spare back room of Gomme's Little Book Shop. It wasn't until 1912 that Frederic and Bertha Goudy were able to rent their own office on Madison Avenue. Other frequent visitors to the book shop included the Pictorial Photographers of America, who held meetings and shared rooms with the book shop for exhibitions. Photographic works by Clarence White, Edward Steichen, and Alvin Langdon Coburn were on permanent display in the shop. These prominent Photo-Secessionists were of great influence on the offshoot group of photographers in Buffalo through their approach to photography as an artistic medium. By this time, Spencer Kellogg had been an active member of the Buffalo Camera Club and the Photo-Pictorialists of Buffalo. In 1912, Kellogg's work was exhibited alongside that of Buffalo and New York Photo-Pictorialists in a New York exhibition organized by Coburn. It is more than likely that Kellogg visited the hub of intellectual activity at the Little Book Shop during trips to New York. His acquaintance with Gomme may have developed from just such a visit, or they may have known each other from other mutual interests. Kellogg's membership in the Grolier and Salmagundi clubs would have kept him in the same circles as Goudy and Gomme in New York. Kellogg no doubt had been a book collector for some time, and the Little Book Shop would have unquestionably been a destination for him even without the Photo-Pictorialist connection. Whether Kellogg met Goudy through this common acquaintance is not certain, but likely. Goudy moved his Village Press to Deepdene Road in Queens in 1914, and later, to Marlboro-on-Hudson. He would eventually connect with Kellogg and the Aries Press as a supplier of type.

In a proclamation that relayed Kellogg's intent, the Aries Book Shop at 116 Delaware Avenue (across from the Statler Hotel), "At the sign of the Ram & Rider," established a tone almost identical to that of the Little Book Shop:

> *The Aries Book Shop is not a commercial book store. We sell books only. Believing that real book lovers prefer to buy in a "booky" place we have tried to create and maintain it.*
> *The books are easily accessible on open shelves and "browsers" are not "badgered." In fact it's the kind of a book shop you've always dreamed about... The Cronies' Room—the coolest spot*

in the summer, a cheerful fire to sit by in the winter—is open
to all patrons who are urged to take advantage of its quiet
atmosphere to select their books at leisure.[12]

The book shop decor and atmosphere was described in detail in an
article from August 1921 entitled "Unique Haven for Bookworm":

One of those "intimate" cozy and friendly sort of book shops
that beckons the book-lover with a warmth like a glowing
hearth has at last been opened in Buffalo. It is the Aries Book
Shop at 116 Delaware and is sponsored solely by Spencer
Kellogg Jr. who upon his retirement from active business, has
seized the first opportunity to establish the "intimate" book
store that he has long felt Buffalo needed.

Taking one of those old brick homes of another day and
remodeling it not too much, so as to preserve the atmosphere
of age, Mr Kellogg first set out to provide as attractive a
setting for his book shop as anyone could desire. He aimed to
make the books appear "at home" and he has succeeded.

The building will soon stand in the shadow of the huge
new Statler hotel across the street—giving one of those sharp
contrasts of ultra-modernity and the quiet seclusion of the
last century. In the front wall has been placed a large show
window that is strongly suggestive of the Colonial period.
The shop is finished in a free Colonial style with grey wood
work and book cases.

A stair case is grey and dull mahogany leads to upper
rooms which are now being prepared for other purposes. The
shop opens into a smaller room in the rear. Here a window
opens on a leafy and somewhat English appearing garden

CORNER OF CRONIES' ROOM

YOU are invited to become a member of the Cronies' Book Club, a Department of the Aries Book Shop organized for the purpose of according to those among its patrons who desire a closer and more co-operative contact, certain unusual and valuable privileges. The seasoned book lover rather than the casual book reader will probably take advantage of this offer, but it is the wish of the club that through its agency, the latter may eventually be converted into true bibliophiles.

THE Cronies' Book Club offers the following special privileges:

Members are put on a preferred mailing list, receiving frequently special literature, reviews, etc.

Members to receive Aries Magazine as published, free of charge.

Members orders—when out of town—forwarded postage free.

Members to receive a five percent discount for cash on book purchases.

Cronies' Book Club Members are offered the use of the Cronies' Room at the Aries Book Shop, cool in the summer; open fire in winter.

Full information relative to the Club may be had from Miss E. B. Sears, Secy, 116 Delaware Ave., Buffalo, N. Y.

[28]

A page from the *Aries* magazine advertising the Cronies' Book Club.

yard. On the walls above book shelves are several fine paintings, wood-block posters and several artistic photographs of
Mr. Kellogg's own workmanship.

In the small hallway where the staircase rises stands
a bronze bust of Emerson by Daniel Chester French, noted
New England Sculptor, the gift of Mrs. Spencer Kellogg Sr.
But the most unique and probably most attractive feature
of the Aries Book Shop is the reading room, located off of the
rear of the store. It has been named the "Cronies' Room."
There is a fireplace that is not purely an ornament. The room
is done in old English style with plain paneled walls finished
in a warm hue. A table, writing desk, lounge and several
chairs—all befitting the room—and a rug or two, constitute
the furnishings. Here, too, are a few decorations including a
painting of a Chinese priest, said by Mr. Kellogg to be about
400 years old, a few long stemmed clay pipes in a wall rack
and one or two other tasteful bits of artistic decoration.

On every hand are book-filled shelves. The book lover is
invited to make the reading room his room. That's what it is
there for, Mr. Kellogg says, and he hopes that it will be much
used. In the same spirit Mr. Kellogg has added a chess table
to the room's furnishings. Smoking is not objected to in the
Cronies' room.

Mr. Kellogg has long been interested in books and art.
His book shop is the realization of a long desire to do something more for Buffalo.

"I have always been a great believer in Buffalo" he
said in relating the story of his new venture. "The city has
long needed one of these book shops the same as it needs a
symphony orchestra and a fine music hall. Rochester and

Cleveland have stores of this kind.

"We don't expect to make money—these kinds of book shops never do. It is our aim to supply the needs of the book lover who has found it necessary to go to New York or else-where to get books that the standard shop could little afford to handle because of the small demand. We are not entering into competition with other book stores. This shop is here to fill an intellectual need of the city."

The shop will be a cultural center, Mr Kellogg believes. He plans to invite noted authors, playwrights, actors and musicians to give informal talks before patrons and guests. On the second floor will be a private tea room for this purpose.

Two other rooms upstairs will be devoted to scarce books and out of print editions. A children's book room may also be fitted out. The shop handles the best of modern literature— American and imported. Many volumes are now on hand and more have been ordered. Since the opening two weeks ago the sales have been encouraging.

The book selections for the shop were made with the assistance of Laurence Gomme of the Neighborhood Bookshop, New York. Great care is being taken in selecting stock.

How did the shop get its name? Mr. Kellogg tells.

"I reached my final decision to establish the shop last April." he said. "That month comes under the zodiacal sign of Aries. The shop was really born under Aries. The name itself is symbolic of high mindedness and intellectuality."[13]

The Aries Book Shop monopolized Kellogg's energies for a few years, until the urge for something more focused replaced them. Beginning with a magazine entitled simply *Aries* and the publication of a book for the Aries Book Club, titled *Niagara*, written by Evelyn M. Watson, the desire to start a full-fledged press was well under way. Various circulars with names such as the *Aries Bookshelf* and *Aries Midsummer 1923* were known to have been produced for the shop.[14] In Volume 2, No. 1 of *Aries* magazine in early 1925, Kellogg announces his vision for the Aries Press:

> *Home of the Aries Press at Eden.*
> *In America as in England a definitely renewed interest is at the present time being taken in fine printing. And not only is this interest being focused upon the making of good books but upon all manner of printing as well: in some instances as much on the part of the purchaser as it is of the producer. Of course the purist rises in majestic wrath when the thought is expressed that "Art" in printing can be applied to commer-cial ends—for that he will claim is impossible and a sacrilege— nevertheless a decided effort is being made on the part of some to give their clients good typography and clean printing. But as Mr. Dwiggins says in a recent article in the Fleuron,[15] so many modern presses have offered specialized services to their clients in the way of writing copy, etc., throwing into the shade their own function as printers, that the technique of printing is liable to be supplanted by the technique of advertising. In this same article Mr. Dwiggins also regrets that the efforts of the more ambitious of the American presses have been and are now directed toward a revival of antique forms rather than toward the evolution of modes and styles suitable for clothing modern ideas in typographic garb. Updike's Merrymount Press he cites as a notable example of one that has attained unquestioned superiority because it has stuck to—printing.*

Emil Georg Sahlin with
the "Ram and Rider" sign
at Aries Press, 2804 East
Church Street, Eden, NY.

But there is another phase and that is the one which
has to do with "private" presses. Here also renewed interest
is apparent. One has only to go to the "rooms" to sense the
change. Press books are climbing. Kelmscott, Dove's [[sic]],
Ashendene, Vale and others are becoming scarcer—at least the
best examples. And Bruce Rogers, still "young and kicking"
hears with amazement the prices paid for books designed by
him. Collectors too are more than ever searching out the fine
Incunabula and early printed books, as well as books about
books, bindings, etc.

So at last we come to ourselves, for we too have come
under the new weavings of the old spell of type and ink and
paper. We have bought a little house on a quiet maple-shaded

street in the town of Eden, N.Y. and there hope to make our dreams come true. We believe in environment.

We love the great outdoors, we believe in the simple life, in the wholesome life in the country. And to us there is no more inspiring country than the rolling and wooded hills about Eden. We have dreamed to print good books beautifully. To express our ideas we felt the Aries Press should grow up in the country.

So we've purchased a press, a lovely thing of gliding movements, of clicking rollers and of polished steel; a wonderful and amazing collection of bright type; cabinets of many drawers to put it in; a host of reglets, wooden furniture, hundreds of pounds of lead, beautiful sweet-smelling paper and a tin or two of ink———

Well, what are we going to print? Wait. We will tell you titles soon enough. But be it understood we shall do our best to make beautiful these new Aries books soon to become realities in the World of Books.

S. Kellogg Jr.[16]

The *Aries* magazine featured interesting insights into the imminent launching of the Aries Press, as well as other fascinating contributions from writers and artists. It contains two illustrations by Rockwell Kent and poems by Gertrude Kellogg Clark (Spencer Jr.'s sister), who was already a published poet.[17] The magazine also contains columns by the book shop's employees,[18] articles on aesthetics and high-minded concerns by Kellogg, and ends with a rather odd clip-out crossword puzzle contest. It also has a two-page spread advertising the Aries Book Shop's stock. This advertisement is an almost identical copy of a sample advertisement seen in the American Type Founders (ATF)

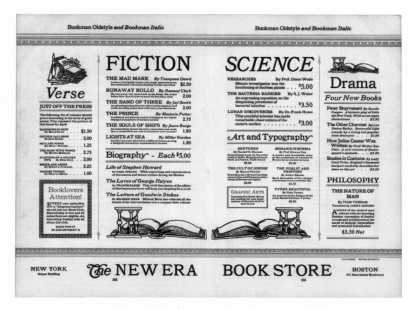

American Type Founders specimen book sample layout,
designed by Emil and/or Axel Sahlin, 1923.

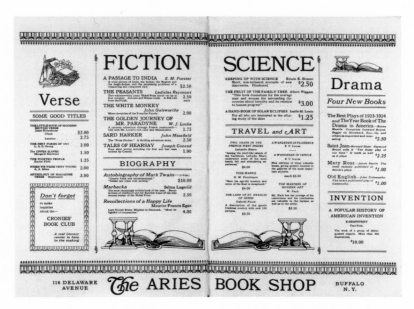

Actual print advertisement for the Aries Book Shop by Emil Georg Sahlin, 1925.

catalog of 1923.[19] The typefaces, ornaments, and arrangement are identical. This was possibly an original layout done first for ATF by Axel or Emil Georg Sahlin,[20] Swedish immigrant brothers who became known for their typographic work at the Roycroft. The typefaces, ornaments and arrangement used in the ATF catalog were then re-appropriated for the Aries layout by Emil Georg Sahlin, who had been hired by Kellogg as his compositor and pressman. It is such an exact copy that it is unlikely that Sahlin would try to pass off a copy of someone else's work as his own. The magazine has no advertisements for any entity other than Aries—the funding and distribution were not those of a traditional magazine. Subscription was a perk for belonging to the Cronies' Book Club. Kellogg's article outlining his aims for the Aries Press are accompanied by a pen and ink illustration of the Aries Press house in Eden, by woodcut artist J.J. Lankes, a Buffalo native. Lankes is most famous for reviving the art of the woodcut in America and for his long-time collaborations of making woodcuts and wood engravings for poet Robert Frost and watercolor artist Charles Burchfield. Kellogg uses a Lankes woodcut from an earlier issue of *Aries magazine* for the *Sweet Cider* broadside of 1926. These Lankes illustrations are not cataloged in Lankes's known works.

One of the most compelling pieces in the *Aries* magazine is a bit of prose entitled "The Spell of the Open Road" by Spencer Kellogg's 16-year-old niece, Martha. This ode to wanderlust speaks of an urgency and energy to live life to its fullest. Martha Kellogg would later start her own art gallery in New York under her married name. Martha Kellogg Jackson and The Martha Jackson Gallery would prove to be pivotal in the cultivation of abstract and pop artists of the late 1950s and '60s.[21]

SWEET CIDER

Apples are red, pumpkins mellow;
Hail with joy each hearty fellow.
Cider runs from frothing presses;
Kiss the maid with golden tresses.
Folly flirts with you and me;
Age comes stumbling o'er the lea.
The time is sped,
The wind is East:
An end must come to every feast.

O.K.
1726
1776
At Peace

Words and design by Spencer Kellogg Jr. Drawing by J. J. Lankes. Two hundred and ten copies, eleven of
them on Japan Vellum signed by the artist and printer, have been set up and privately printed by Spencer
Kellogg Jr at the Aries Press in the Village of Eden, N. Y. Ordinary copies a Quarter, signed copies $1.00.

"Sweet Cider" broadside by Spencer Kellogg Jr., with illustration by J.J. Lankes.

The cottage in Eden where the Press was set up continued with the theme of colonial decor that was a trademark of the Aries Book Shop. A year after the Press was officially launched, the shop was still running but winding down, and yet another plan was in the works. Spencer Kellogg Jr. purchased 200 acres of land along Jennings Road in Eden, New York, with the intention of forming an artists' colony modeled after the McDowell artist colony (an artistic retreat in the White Mountains of New Hampshire), which is still in existence today. In 1927, a mansion was built on the property called Aries Hill, but the artists' colony never materialized. The Aries Press was housed in a smaller location on East Church Street in Eden. The Kelloggs also lived there while the mansion on Aries Hill was being constructed. There is no mention of the Roycroft Campus as a point of comparison for his plans, but there is no doubt that Roycroft influenced how Kellogg envisioned his press and colony, either through deliberately trying to distinguish Aries's own identity, or by avoiding Roycroft for other reasons.

The Roycroft Press

The notion of establishing a private press on the outskirts of Buffalo was not a revolutionary idea. Since 1895, Elbert Hubbard's Roycroft Campus in East Aurora (only a few miles from Eden) was a thriving enterprise. Hubbard was a former executive with the Larkin Soap Company (and mentor to Darwin D. Martin), who reportedly visited William Morris in England, and was inspired to form his own artist/craftsman community in East Aurora, New York. The Roycroft Press produced a huge amount of material from 1895 to 1938. While the deluxe editions of the Roycroft Press were inspired and well made, most of the print materials were mass-produced and arguably contrary to the ideals of the Arts and Crafts movement. Morris purists often disregard the Roycroft as a bastardization of the Morris ideal. Morris's own daughter, May, declined an invitation to visit the Roycroft because it would dignify "...that obnoxious imitator of my father."[22] While Hubbard imitated Morris in many ways, he came closer to Morris's socialist leanings. The Kelmscott Press made

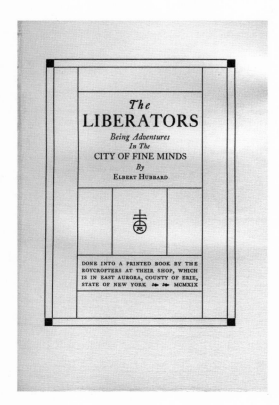

The title page for *The Liberators* designed by Axel Sahlin for the Roycrofters in 1919. His design was a distinct departure from the early William Morris affectations of the Roycroft style.

expensive editions and only the wealthy could afford Morris's books, while Hubbard made his publications accessible to all strata of society. Despite decidedly mixed reviews, the Roycrofters's legacy of work demands attention, and to this day commands collector premiums. Some of the finer editions of the Roycroft books featured Dard Hunter designs and the typography of Axel and Emil Georg Sahlin. Hunter gave the Roycroft its most distinctive graphic legacy with illustrations and title lettering that was as much influenced by Viennese modernism as it was by Morris's pre-Raphaelite sensibilities. Axel Sahlin was instrumental in helping the Roycroft develop its own typographic style away from the heavy William Morris influence. Axel had emigrated from Sweden in 1911 to work as a printer at the Roycroft. His younger brother Emil followed three years later, and both carried on their father's trade as artisan printers.

Kellogg's vision for Aries Press was more than simply creating a vanity press for his own writing, which was undeniably a part of his motivation. It would have been much less trouble to have other printers produce his volumes with him as a commercial client on a job-by-job basis. Kellogg's father and sister had books published by Grabau Bindery[23] in Buffalo, and the Roycroft had begun to do more work-for-hire job-printing in the time after the death of Elbert Hubbard and his wife (tragically in the 1915 sinking of the RMS *Lusitania*). By the time Kellogg started the Aries Press, Roycroft was living off Hubbard's legacy. However, without Hubbard's guidance, it lacked a strong direction and eventually closed operations in 1938—one more victim of the Depression. Echoing Roycrofter sentiments concerning the Arts and Crafts movement, Kellogg said in a newspaper interview years after closing the Aries Press:

> *I think there is a place in the world and a useful job for the man who produces beautiful things. I realize that I am no genius or artist myself but if my work and expenditure aided others in production of something of lasting beauty I would conclude that I have succeeded. I am not a medievalist and I have no grievance against the present or its methods, but after all the great satisfaction in doing a thing was taken away when it became unnecessary to do it with our own hands. The wonder is that there are craftsmen still in our trades. At the Aries Press we are going to take advantage of the best talent we can obtain whether from near or afar.*[24]

Kellogg put this sentiment into action by hiring away Roycroft typographer Emil Georg Sahlin as his compositor and pressman. Sahlin was a true craftsman who regarded printing with great reverence: he even referred to each piece of type as a "jewel."[25]

In the shadow of the Roycroft, it would be difficult to start a press that would seem anything more than an imitation of its established neighbor. Kellogg managed to do at least two things that would make the Aries Press more Kelmscott-like than the Roycrofters had managed. William Morris literally put his life into his work (he died in 1896, the year his most famous book, the Kelmscott Chaucer, was finished). Morris saw to every detail of his work, from the writing to the printing. He even designed his own typefaces, as there were none available that he found suitable for his work. Even with the large volume of work produced at the Roycroft, they never produced their own fonts—they used commercially available typefaces. This is no shame; producing a proprietary typeface was an extremely time-consuming and expensive process. Kellogg pursued this lofty goal of having his own type by commissioning one from none other than Frederic W. Goudy, and later on, Kellogg would also purchase Morris's Albion Press from Goudy.

Frederic W. Goudy and the Aries Type

Frederic W. Goudy (1865–1947) created more than 100 typefaces during his lifetime. Like most type designers, his name is known to a more general audience through eponymously titled faces such as Goudy Text and Goudy Oldstyle. Goudy's work ranged from widely used faces made for the Lanston Monotype Corporation to private commissions that few people have ever seen. Although lost in the sense that it was not well known, Aries was not one of the "Lost Goudy Types"[26] that perished in a fire at his Deepdene studio in 1939.

When Goudy started up his business of selling his own typefaces through his Village Letter Foundery [sic], he found Kellogg to be a very good customer. Kellogg also commissioned Goudy to cut a proprietary typeface for his new Aries Press. The history of the Aries face is somewhat confused since it was later modified and renamed for another client. The Aries type was cast in one size: 16

HAHBHCHCHDHEHEHFHG
HHIHJHNHOHPHQHRHSH
HTHℒH·COMOBOCOCODO
OEOEOFOGOHOIOJONOOO
OPOQOROSOTOℒCPRINT

mambmcmdmemfmgmhmimkmlm
mnmompmqmrmsmtmumvmwmr
mymzm?m/mflm Aries Press

CTHen this lady sayde suffer me to go

First Proof of Aries Type with hand written note by Frederic Goudy.

THE ELEVENTH BOOK. CINCIDIT CAPITULUM PRIMUM
How Syr Launcelot rode on his adventure, & how he helpe a dolorous lady fro
hyr payne, and how he faught with a Dragon.

NOW leve we Syr Tristram de Lyones, & speak we of sire Launcelot du
Lake & of sire Galahalt, syr Launcelots sone, hou he was goten, and in
what maner as the book of Frensshe rehcrceth. Afore the tyme that syr
Galahalt was borne, there came in an hermyte vnto Kynge Arthur vpon whyt-
sonday, as the knyghtes satte at the table round; and whan the hermyte sawe the
syege perillous, he asked the kyng & alle the knyghtes why that sege was voyd?

This proof shows the Aries type, designed by Frederic Goudy for Mr. Spencer
Kellogg Jr., before final revision as to line & weight. Marlboro, N.Y., Dec. 19—
ABCCDEEFGHIJKLMNOODQQRSTUVYZ&
Cabcdefghiklmnopqrstuvwxyzctffl;?!.,-{1234567890}(æ)

Advanced stage of Aries Type design with final notations in pencil by Goudy
Both images from Frederic W. Goudy Collection,
Special Collections Research Center, Syracuse University Libraries.

point[27]. Like the William Morris Troy type, it is a stylized roman with blackletter characteristics. It was partially inspired by a type created by Emery Walker for the Ashendene Press (1900). Walker's Subiaco type was based on a type of the same name designed by two German monks: Conrad Sweynheym and Arnold Pannartz (1465). Subiaco is often credited as a key development towards a true roman type or "a font well on the way thereto."[28] Created by two Germans at a press in Italy, this seems perfectly appropriate.

The Aries type was used in only one known book, *In Praise of My Lady* by William Morris (1928). Shortly afterward, Kellogg abandoned his press and the type was forgotten. Goudy was not fully satisfied with his design for Aries and chose to re-cut many characters for his own private use. This re-cut font was named Village Text. The Grabhorn Press of San Francisco admired this face and in 1931 persuaded Goudy to sell them the design. They renamed this new typeface Franciscan. Goudy tells the story of the lineage of these faces in his book *A Half-Century of Type Design and Typography*,[29] however the sample specimen used for Aries is actually a piece hand set by Bertha Goudy using Village Text (Franciscan). The Aries face is nearly unknown to even the most knowledgeable typophiles due to misidentification by Goudy himself. It could be forgiven that Goudy was not completely accurate in recalling his own work, since he was in his eighties and fell ill during the course of the book's production. This specimen is used as the only known source of Aries.

The two faces, Aries and Franciscan (Village Text) are very similar, but several characters have striking differences. Subsequent surveys of Goudy's work perpetuated this misidentification. Cross-reference of various Goudy books might confirm that this shown specimen

Aries (top) and Franciscan (bottom) types shown each with subtle differences between them.

Page extract from *Divinae institutiones of Lactantius* (1465), showing Subiaco typeface used by Pannartz and Sweynheym in 1465. Image courtesy of the Newberry Library, Chicago, IL.

was in fact Aries when in actuality it is not. The example printed in the *Half-Century* is Aqua Vitae and is correctly cited in Melbert Cary's *A Bibliography of the Village Press, 1903-1938.*[30] With additional research done at the Cary Collection at the Rochester Institute of Technology, Village Text was clearly identified as the source credited as Aries in *Half-Century* .

While Goudy had already developed a reputation as a great type designer, his Aries type was his first venture into the full process of matrix engraving and type founding. Up until that time, Goudy had designed his faces, and then handed the drawings over to craftsmen (most often Robert Wiebking) who finished and cast the type through large type foundries such as Lanston Monotype and American Type Founders. The development of the face and its story are recalled by Goudy in *Half-Century:*

ARIES [Design No. 54]

SHORTLY *after beginning work at my newly-established Village Letter Foundry in 1925, Spencer Kellogg, of Eden, New York, began operating his new private press, and for it he placed large orders for types I was casting and offering to printers—in fact, his orders embarrassed me by their size, as I was not as yet equipped for large output.*

On one of Kellogg's visits to Marlboro, he suggested that he might like a private type for his "Aries Press." My first thought was to make for him a letter based upon the classic forms of the early Venetians, and sketches were begun along this line and approved by him, but on the occasion of a later visit to my workshop, a suggestion was made whether by me

AQUA VITAE

ONE Theoricus wrote a proper treatise of *Aqua Vitae*, wherein he praiseth it unto the ninth degree. He distinguisheth three sorts thereof, *simplex, composita, & Perfectissima*. He declareth the simples and ingrediences thereunto belonging. He wisheth it to be taken as well before meat as after. It drieth up the breaking out of hands and killeth the flesh wormes, if you wash your hands therewith.

IT SCOWRETH all scurfe and scalds from the head, being therewith dailie washt before meales. Being moderatlie taken [saith he] it sloweth age, it strengtheth youth, it helpeth digestion, it cutteth flegme, it lighteneth the mind, it quickeneth the spirits, it cureth the hydropsie, it healeth the Strangurie, it pounceth the stone, it expelleth gravel, it puffeth aways all ventositie, it keepeth and preserveth the head from whirling, the eies from dazeling, the toong from lisping, the mouth from masfling, the teeth from chattering, and the throte from ratling; it keepeth the weasan from stifling, the stomach from wambling, and the heart from swelling, the bellie from wirtching, the guts from numbling, the hands from shivering, & the sinews from shrinking, the veines from crumpling, the bones from aking, and the marrow from soaking. Ulstadius also ascribeth thereto a singular praise and would have it to burne being kindled which he taketh to be a token to know the goodness thereof. And trulie it is a soverigne liquor if it be orderlie taken.

REPRINTED FROM HOLINSHED'S CHRONICLES (1577) IN THIS
CONTROVERSIAL YEAR OF OUR LORD M DCCCC XXXII FOR
THE FRIENDS OF FREDERIC & BERTHA GOUDY
MARLBOROUGH, NEW YORK

Aqua Vitae printed by Bertha Goudy using the redesigned Aries type, then called Village Text.

or by him, I do not remember—that a type with some quali-
ties not generally found in the early Italian types might be
a pleasing variation, since the type he wanted was intended
for printing texts in limited editions, texts that in themselves
would not be ordinary.

We talked over the types of the private presses and
finally decided that a face with the color and mass effect of the
Subiaco used by St. John Hornby at his famous Ashendene
Press was the sort that offered possibilities for a new letter.
The first sketches I had made for a roman thereupon were
scrapped and drawings for a new "old face" were begun. This
was in the summer of 1925.

I had purchased an engraving machine; I could not
purchase also the mechanical knack needed to use it, a knack
which comes only from experience; so it was a really chancy
undertaking for me to attempt (with no previous matrix
cutting experience) the engraving of a hundred or more
matrices. Records of progress at this time were not kept
consistently, but by noting dates that occasionally appeared
on drawings or proofs, I find that my first pencil drafts are
dated November 8, 1925, and by November 22 my drawings
in ink were completed. And then began the travail of
accomplishment.

Drawings were easy to make, but how to translate
drawings into patterns from which to cut matrices? Some
sort of pattern was essential, and a record of those I
attempted shows that more than one hundred and fifty
were made; at first some letters were cut laboriously from
hard fibre sheets about one-sixteenth of an inch thick, which
were then mounted with Lepage's glue on other sheets of

the same fibre, making enlarged sunken patterns for use
in producing reduced metal working patterns; for others,
letters were cut from heavy Bristol board and likewise
mounted, but this material proved not too satisfactory. I
finally found that a hard drawing paper, three or four ply,
gave me the best results, and I have used it for all of my
master-pattern work since.

Then came the matter of grinding engraving tools that
would cut a sunken matrix in hard brass or German silver
fifty-odd thousandths of an inch deep; the preparation of
the matrix blanks; the thousand and one things necessary
before a single matrix could be cut; and the repeated experi-
ments, all of which required considerable time—so that it
was well into 1926 before I was able to show proofs of some
seventy characters.

As might be expected, these first proofs showed
inequalities in weight, line, etc., yet on the whole I believe
they were probably as successful as the first efforts of many
of the early craftsmen starting from scratch." Corrections,
recuttings, changes, took time, and my customer, tiring
of his press in the meantime, shut up shop—throwing the
type back on my hands. What finally became of the 500-odd
pounds of 16-point type I had shipped to him, I do not know.

The information contained in this account of the Aries
face has been taken from notes prepared prior to the fire in
1939. I have written at length because the work on this face
represents the principal beginnings of my typefounding experience, and until now has never been put into print.[31]

Goudy further elaborates on the type design later in the book:

FRANCISCAN [Design No. 81]

FRANCISCAN is the name given by Edwin Grabhorn to
the redesigned and recut Aries face (Design No. 54). Grabhorn
had purchased the face after seeing a proof of it on the occasion
of my visit to his shop in San Francisco in 1931. I had
renamed the Aries face "Village Text," and intended to use it
for my own printing rather than to offer it for general sale.
   Grabhorn first used it for printing The Spanish
Occupation of California, in February 1934. This book took
highest honors at the American Institute of Graphic Arts
"Fifty Books of the Year" exhibition that year. It was also
used to print the Grabhorn Press Bibliography, in 1940. I am
not sure in my own mind that this type was the best that
might have been selected for this bibliography, even though
it was my design and the property of the Press; but I believe
it to be well adapted for reprints of matter leaning toward
the archaic. In Grabhorn's use of it for the Book Club of
California's folio about the first edition of the King James
Bible, with a genuine 1611 leaf included, I can find no fault.
The type adapts itself beautifully to a two-column page.
   The matrices were electrotyped by the Monotype
Company from my redesigned types and cast for Grabhorn
by McKenzie and Harris, San Francisco.[32]

In 1924, Frederic Goudy had acquired from James Guthrie of the
Pear Tree Press in Sussex, England, the actual Kelmscott Albion
press that William Morris had used to print his famous Chaucer.

Cover of Aries Press prospectus booklet with woodcut by James Guthrie.

Kellogg mentioned that he had an opportunity to purchase the Kelmscott press in 1921, but because of his time being dedicated to opening the Aries Book Shop, he had to decline. James Guthrie later contributed a striking woodcut illustration for the cover of an Aries Press booklet in 1926. Kellogg was able to purchase the Kelmscott Albion from Fred Goudy only a year after it was obtained from Guthrie. Why Goudy parted with the press is not clear, but he did have another Albion at the Village Press[33], and Kellogg must have made an enticing offer. According to Melbert Cary, Spencer Kellogg "was able to persuade Mr. Goudy to part with the Press"[34] in the summer of 1925. But printing historian, and later owner of the Albion, J. Ben Lieberman puts it more frankly: "Mr. Kellogg had bought the Albion from Mr. Goudy, who desperately needed money to keep his type-designing activities going."[35] With the possession of its own typeface and an actual Kelmscott printing press, the Aries Press was truly an heir to the spirit of William Morris.

Only one book produced by Kellogg and Sahlin used the Aries typeface and was also printed on the Kelmscott Albion press. It was a very limited edition book entitled *In Praise of My Lady* by William Morris, printed in 1928. All of the other books and ephemera of the Press from 1925 to 1928 used other typefaces. Aside from the typography, Kellogg's publications also featured work by book artists such as Rockwell Kent and children's book illustrators Wanda Gág and Elizabeth MacKinstry.

Books from the Aries Press

The first book published under the actual Aries Press imprint, *The Ghost Ship* (1926), had a simple elegance, yet felt much more substantial than the 20 pages that the story occupies. The book was set in English Caslon type on English handmade paper. This may well be in a conspicuous deference to the author being English. The boards were wrapped in a deep blue marbled paper flecked with metallic gold swirls, and appropriately evocative of the subject matter of the book. The tasteful ornamentation and pristine presswork surely helped it win the honor of being chosen for the AIGA 50 Books Award of 1926. The next book, completed in March 1927, *The Oak by the Waters of Rowan* is a little less restrained, with somewhat mismatched typefaces and illustrations by children's book illustrator Wanda Gág. The subtle leaf pattern papers on the cover boards have almost the same deep intensity as *The Ghost Ship*, but its variance in size and hue are enough to differentiate it from a matched house style. In fact none of the five Aries books share the same dimensions, typefaces, or decorative treatments. The next book, *Verses*, completed in January 1928, featured the poetry of Kellogg's sister, Gertrude. The paper boards sport a cubist-inspired airbrushed array of overlapping shapes in hues of red and green. This is surprisingly subtle, and works with the delicate italic poetry settings inside. This book garnered a second AIGA 50 Books Award for 1928. March of 1928 produced the fourth book by Kellogg and Sahlin. *Little Songs by the Way* is another poetry book, this one made as a gift for Kellogg's daughter in a small edition of 95 copies. The final book, *In Praise of My Lady* by William Morris, was printed in April 1928 in the

Top: Cover and title page for *Verses* by Gertrude Kellogg Clark.

Bottom: Two sample layout pages for *Verses*. Many other variations of printed and hand drawn trial title pages exist in Scripps College collection.

smallest stated edition of any Aries item, only 31 copies. The small print run may indicate that the market was not clamoring for what Kellogg was producing. This last book featured the Aries type and illustrations by Elizabeth MacKinstry. This book is the largest in dimension of any Aries book (8.5" × 13") but has only six printed pages and no title page. The green marble boards quarter-bound over leather appear to be an oil marbling, which has a curious coarse-ness and lacks the elegance found in the previous Aries books.

Four Short Years

The Aries Press existed for nearly four years, with accolades coming from many sources. For example, Bruce Rogers gave a backhanded compliment by acknowledging receipt of presswork from Aries:

> Thanks very much for the Memorial Pamphlet which you were kind enough to send me. It is quite beyond reproach tech-nically. You are to be congratulated on having attained such perfect printing in so short a time. If I say that I don't alto-gether care for the design of it, as a whole, you will, I think, understand that it is just my finicking [sic] personal dissatis-faction with most modern printing, my own included.[36]

Kellogg reached out to luminaries on both sides of the Atlantic to collaborate and make his presence known, traveling to England to meet with William Morris's daughter, May, as well as Emery Walker, C. H. St. John Hornby, and other notable figures of the British fine press world.[37]

In 1928, Emil Georg Sahlin was asked to join his brother Axel in his new business, Sahlin Typographic Service. Either due to the resignation of Sahlin or simply because he had grown weary of the demands of the Press, Kellogg closed the doors to Aries.[38] After shutting down the Press, Kellogg turned his attentions to living the good life and indulging his inclinations as an artist. Occasional articles in society columns give some clue as to how his time was spent. A September 1933 newspaper article discussed his painting endeavors and his studio at Derby-on-the-Lake near Buffalo. In ensuing years, Kellogg visited studios in New York, Italy, and California. His daughter Lois joined him in his Paris studio as she was finishing a book of poems published by the Mosher Press of Maine.[39] The unnamed author of an article in the Buffalo *Courier Express* described Kellogg's paintings as "Imaginative fantasies, they have a restful far away quality, a mystic and dreamlike feeling, that is as pleasant as a mild drug."[40] The article continued about his imminent plans to travel to Tunisia to paint "a large number of nudes" with the added caveat from Kellogg: "just imagine...catching the glint of exquisite mahogany and walnut skin, lit up with the clear light of the tropical sun—imagine the classical contours of the pure-bred and proud native bodies with the most colorful background in the world. It's a painter's paradise, and I expect to achieve something really great while there."[41]

In 1935 he and his wife took their yacht to Alaska on a hunting and fishing trip. It was shortly after that time when Kellogg divorced his first wife and married a much younger woman: Cosette Kupp[42]. They moved to California to start a new life with an adopted child. In the early 1940s, Kellogg visited Scripps College and was impressed with their students and library. He donated many of his fine press books (from Kelmscott, Doves, and Bruce Rogers, among others) to the library[43]. He also donated many examples of test proofs for the *Verses* book as well as dozens of studies for an unfinished book entitled "Marsh Poems" and other Aries books, working proofs, and correspondence.[44] Kellogg was invited but was unable to attend the dedication of the new Scripps College typeface in 1941. He sent his regrets that he was not able to join the festivities with the college and the type's designer, Mr. Goudy.[45]

Emil Georg Sahlin's Work

It is not clear how the socialite Kellogg met Sahlin, who was clearly a working-class man, but Kellogg may have been aware of Sahlin's skillful work that he had done at the Roycroft, and sought him out as his compositor. After leaving Kellogg and the Aries Press in 1928, Emil Georg Sahlin continued to work as a printer and teacher until his death in 1983. The following is an account of Emil's life as a printer. Multiple drafts of a lecture given by Mr. Sahlin were compiled and some editing was done, but most information remains in his voice as written by Sahlin.[46]

> *Emil Georg Sahlin was born in one of the oldest cities in Sweden, named Lund, one of the university cities. Graduated from Teachers Seminary. My first job was in one of the finest jewelry stores in the city. Nelson's Royal Jewelers. Mr. Nelson thought I had a good hand in drawing and wanted to send me to Jenson's in Copenhagen to study. Being too young*

I really didn't know what I wanted to do. I spent two years at Nelson's. Then I took a job as bellhop and switchboard operator at Grand Hotel. I thought that it would be something different and [that I would] meet a lot a people from all over the world so I took the job. After two years there I couldn't see much future and decided it was about time to learn a trade. Although many times did I say to myself that I would never become a printer as I had watched my father standing there setting type and building pictures with rules and ornaments, but since both my father and brother were printers I decided to follow in their footsteps.

In the year of 1910 my brother Axel had a printing magazine named "NORDISK BOOKTRYCK" where there were [sic] a write-up about Elbert Hubbard and the Roycroft Shops located in East Aurora, New York, it had several illustrations showing the print shop and other crafts, he thought it would be a very interesting place to visit and perhaps hoping that Mr. Hubbard would put him to work. So the following year 1911 he made up his mind to make the trip and see some of America. [Upon his] Arrival in New York he visited the American Type Founders where they put him to work on their large Type specimen book. Made his first dollars there, then on to see our Uncle in Boston, Mass. He visited the city and found a fine looking mint shop named Lincoln Smith where they put him to work. After a stay there with a little more dollars decided to make the trip to East Aurora, New York. Upon arrival he stayed at the Inn. At the time Mr. Hubbard was expected back the following day from a lecture tour. Met Hubbard and soon got acquainted with him, and told him his reason for coming from Sweden to meet Mr. Hubbard and see his Roycroft shops that he read about, so he showed him some of his work which impressed Mr. Hubbard so much that he put him right to work with so much pay and room and board at the Inn. Hubbard was so impressed with his work that he decided to drop the Morris style and gave Axel a free hand—so from that time on it was Sahlin's Typography and impressions that changed the Roycroft style—that went so good with printing sales men brought back all kinds of work from the four corners of America. So then Axel became a typographic artist and designer and later became the superintendent of the composing room.

In 1914 he decided to take a months vacation to go back home for a visit. We were all very happy to see him after 3 years away from home. With him he brought back many fine books that he has designed and several pieces of copper and leather articles made by the Roycroft Craftsmen.

At the time I was learning the printing trade at the famous Brotherna Forsell's Boktryckeri in the city of Malmo where Axel once also worked, and only had one year to finish my trade and graduate as printers journeyman. I made up my mind hoping that Axel would take me back with him so I decided to see the city clerk about taking out my papers to go to America which I did. At the time war was declared and Axel got notice from the Cunard line that his trip had to be cut short to be able to cross the Atlantic. As he had his trip received on the Cunard Line LACONIA from Liverpool England, So I said Axel please take me back with you, then he said you can't go as you have to serve your 3 years in the Army, so I said no I don't. Why?- because I have already taken my papers out to leave for America. Then he said have you any money? No but I will pay you when I start working for Elbert Hubbard. After eleven days on the Atlantic crossing from Liverpool to New York we had a very exciting and experienced trip across the Atlantic. We zigzagged further north than any passenger ships had ever gone. We were chased by submarines a couple of times, this we did not find out before our landing in New York. Big headlines on the newspapers "Laconia arrives with thousands of passengers safe" Laconia laid in New York three days and was ready to go back again, and on her third day out she was torpedoed and sunk by a German submarine.

So finally we arrived back in East Aurora. I was very impressed with the little village, and seeing all the beautiful Roycroft buildings which were just like the ones I saw in the Swedish printers magazine. The next day I for the first time met Elbert Hubbard and I took a liking to him right away even if I could not speak or understand him as I did not understand English, and the first thing I did was taking a picture of him and my brother Axel and how I had wished now that Axel would turned around and had my picture with him. as I never did get a chance for that moment again.

Elbert Hubbard put me to work right away. Took me a little time to learn the way the type cases were laid as they were different from ours in Sweden, but it did not take me long to learn that. I was used to set different languages in Sweden, and it did not take me long to learn the English. I lived with my brother at the Inn for a time and during that time we were about eight of us at the breakfast, lunch and dinner table. When Miss Lillian Hanley Gerhart who was

Mr. Hubbards concert pianist at the Inn taught me all the
names of the things used at the table and food, and what
I liked the best for breakfast was Corn Flakes and Cream
and the [...] and food were mostly from the Roycroft farm. I
progressed far in my work and became top typographer at the
shop, and I happened to be a rather good tennis player and
every time guests came at the Inn and wanted to play tennis.
Elbert Hubbard called to lay down my composers sticks and
come out and play tennis with one of our guests. I loved
Elbert and Alice Hubbard very much and to this day I still
say it were the best eleven years of my life.

    In 1925 I left Roycroft to operate the private Aries press
for Spencer Kellogg, Jr., in Eden New York. Two of the books
I designed, set and printed there were included among the
"Fifty Best Books" of their years. The original press used by
William Morris in printing his famous Kelmscott Chaucer
was owned by the Aries Press. I stayed there for three years.
In 1928, upon the invitation of my brother, I began to work
at the Axel Edward Sahlin Typographic Service, the first
typographic service in Buffalo producing high-grade advertising
typography for the trade. After my brother passed away I
operated the shop until 1965.

    I married Julia Conrad and we are still happy together,
and I am working every day at the Paradise Press in Buffalo.
As Elbert Hubbard always said "work is the best medicine.[47]

Sahlin's life as a printer was only one aspect of his colorful life. He
was very athletic as his proclivity for tennis implies. In Sweden he
played soccer and participated as a long-distance runner in the 1912
Stockholm Olympics. He was a figure skater in the Buffalo Skating

Club for 11 years. During his tenure at the Aries Press, Sahlin also conducted a seven-piece dance orchestra. His hobby of making modeled copper foil relief sculptures may have been a lasting influence from his time at the Roycroft and its renowned copper shop.

Civilité Orchestra, circa 1927, led by Emil Georg Sahlin on drums.

Unfinished Work

In a letter to an unknown inquirer,[48] Emil Georg Sahlin obliged for some history of the Aries Press by paraphrasing the "Recapitulation of the first year" and offered that only three books were printed at the Press: *The Ghost Ship*, *The Oak by the Waters of Rowan*, and *A Book of Poems by Lois Kellogg*. (At least five books credit Sahlin in the colophon, so his recollection was hazy.) He also mentioned that several keepsakes were printed for the Aries Book Club. Sahlin stated that he "had several other books in the making"[49] for Aries that were never finished. These were:

- William Morris, "Ogier the Dane" from *The Earthly Paradise*
- Sidney Lanier, *Sunrise and the Marshes of Glynn, Two Poems*
- Edgar Allan Poe, five selected poems, including the "Three Nocturnes"

All three of these books are listed in the recapitulation of the first year as "Works now under consideration" along with "Prose selections

& poems from the great Nature lovers such as BURROUGHS, WHITMAN, THOREAU and the like," and "Completion of the 'American' Rhyme Sheet series." Other works, which were considered but never materialized, were Marcel Schob's *Mimes* and José-Maria Heredia's *The Trophies*.

For *The Marsh Poems* by Sidney Lanier, Kellogg enlisted J.J. Lankes to provide two illustrations and an ornament. Despite proofs being pulled, technical problems, and the imminent departure of Sahlin on April 15, 1928, this project was left to remain unfinished. This time also saw Kellogg beginning to disperse his print shop through selling Lankes an etching press.[50]

The book entitled *The Legend of the Rich Man and the Jew* is listed in the 1926 booklet *Recapitulation of the First Year* as "TO BE READY SHORTLY" along with *The Oak by the Waters of Rowan*. *The Oak* of course was issued, but even though the *Rich Man* is mentioned in articles, letters, order blanks, and the 1926 booklet, there is no evidence that it was ever finished. In a letter to Wilbur Macy Stone in 1926, Kellogg relays his progress on the book and his hiring of Allen Lewis to illustrate the book.

> *Dear Mr. Stone,*
>
> *Again I am forced to write a letter of regrets owing to my failure to accept your kind invitation to come down to see you at the Park Row Building. It seems that I never come to New York without a date book so full of appointments that I never quite succeed in checking them all off. It was absolutely impossible for me to take the time to get down to your office and back. My daughter and Mrs. Kellogg were with me and*

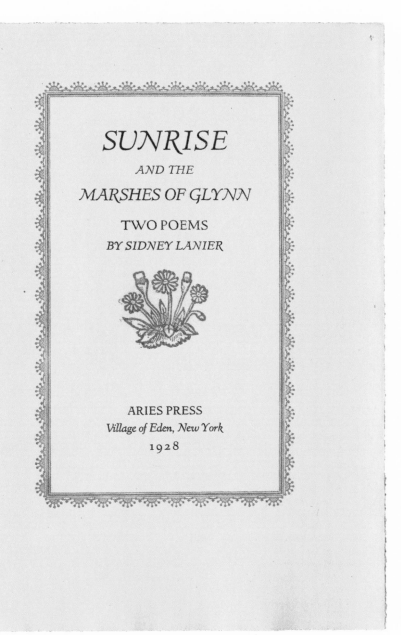

SUNRISE

AND THE

MARSHES OF GLYNN

TWO POEMS

BY SIDNEY LANIER

ARIES PRESS
Village of Eden, New York
1928

Lanier's title page with J.J. Lankes's woodcut.
Image courtesy of the Ella Strong Denison Library, Scripps College.

Owners of the Kelmscott Goudy Albion Press
(Hopkinson & Cope Improved Albion Press No. 6551)

Frederic W. Goudy with the William Morris Press
at the Anderson Galleries, New York, photograph by Arnold Genthe, 1924.

William Morris - Kelmscott Press 1895–1898

C.R. Ashbee - Essex House Press 1898–1913

Washington Herbert Broome - The Old Bourne Press 1913–1920

Miss Nellie Platt (Broome's Secretary) 1920

James Guthrie - Pear Tree Press 1920–1924

Frederic Goudy - Village Press 1924–1925

Spencer Kellogg Jr - Aries Press 1925–1932

Melbert Cary Jr - Press of the Woolly Whale 1932–1941

George Van Vechten 1941–1960

J. Ben Lieberman and Elizabeth Koller Lieberman - Herity Press 1961–2001

Jethro K. Lieberman 2001–2013

RIT Cary Graphic Arts Collection 2013–Present

there was something doing every minute.

Thanks for your kindness in sending Allen Lewis's address. I had the pleasure of meeting him and he accepted the commission to do a couple of illustrations for my essay "The Legend of the Rich Man and the Jew." I hope that he likes the story and that the doing of the work is giving him some pleasure. If the drawings are soon ready, I hope to be able to have the book on the press some time in January.

With kind regards, I beg to remain

Yours Sincerely
Spencer Kellogg[51]

A few years later after the Aries Press has ceased operations, Wilbur Macy Stone writes to Spencer Kellogg:

August 15, 1930
My Dear S.K. Jr. — For a number of years I have been making a small annual contribution to the Children's Village at Dobbs Ferry. I have never been there but I always feel that helping the youngsters is more profitable than any other betterment effort, so I am particularly drawn to work among children.

I was delighted to discover in a recent booklet from the Children's Village the report of your splendid gift of printing equipment.

It gave me a real thrill and I congratulate—and envy you.
Sincerely,[52]

Kellogg responds in September 1930:

My Dear Mr. Stone,

    Very Few people now-a-days find the time—even though they have the inclinations—to write thoughtful letters as you have done. To say I appreciate your kindness in writing me about the shop at Children's Village would be putting it mildly. Many, many thanks.

    As to my own work at the press I have become somewhat discouraged through my inability to find a good man, as assistant, since Sahlin accepted a very fine offer to go work with his brother ⟦in⟧ a commercial venture as "Typographer" in Buffalo. As I have been writing for years, and ⟦lately⟧ find that I enjoy more completely the directly creative work of "verse working", which will not permit me to undertake the actual physical labor of going on with the press alone. I have practically decided to count the ⟦printing⟧ as a valuable experience in the appreciation of fine typography and discontinue ⟦definitely⟧ the actual "business" connected with a private press—buying, selling, circularaizing, collecting, corresponding, etc—is unbelievably arduous; and the returns, compared with expenses, practically nil. I hope the Gods will forgive me because I do not choose to longer tread the thorny path of achievement in this particular line.

Yours Sincerely
Spencer Kellogg[53]

It is not known what equipment was donated, but it is possible that that Aries type was included in that donation. The Children's Village did have a printing program, but further research into the fate of the Aries press donation vanished with a 1994 fire in their administration building, which destroyed all records and archives. The fate of the Kelmscott Albion press is well documented in the book *The Liberty Bell on the Kelmscott Goudy Press*[54]:

Kellogg produced one last book[55] the year he died (1944). This book is a basic volume of his poetry, lacking in the overall attention to paper, printing, and binding details that might confuse it with other Aries books. It was published by the Schauer Printing Studio in Santa Barbara, California, which appears to have been an occasional publisher of books. The poems range from sentimental verse to the darker poem entitled "Ennui" ("The world rolls on indifferent to me"). The undated poems are arranged by title alphabetically and often carry locations: Paris, Florence, Eden, Exeter, New York, Arizona, Villa Pazzi, Tahoe... giving some clue to the years compiled in the book. Kellogg died of a heart attack on December 20, 1944.

Ultimately, Kellogg was a mysterious figure with a variety of artistic interests. The extant evidence suggests his vision to produce the finest press work was possibly only realized with the abilities of Emil Georg Sahlin. It is telling that he completely gave up the Press after Sahlin left. Sahlin was clearly a craftsman who took pride in his own work ethic, and in recalling his departure from Aries, he said,

> *Mr. Spencer Kellogg didn't like it. He wrote a little note for me to send by the chauffer, he said, "Emil, I thought you worked for the art and not for the money." I returned the letter and told him, "Mr. Spencer Kellogg, if I had your money and everything, it would be different, but I'm a working man and I need it. This is a little bit too slow a thing.*

I only do a book a year and it's tiresome and everything, so I had to do something worthwhile," and I did.[56]

The brief existence of Aries Press is only one of many fine press ventures with a few curious twists and connections to the wider printing and book worlds. The books and ephemera produced by Kellogg and Sahlin stand out as notable examples of early 20th-century American fine presswork. The special collections at the Denison Library show that Kellogg worked on many trial sketches and printed multiple detailed test proof pages with minute variations—almost to a point of indecision and crippling obsessive overthinking.[57] The Emil Georg Sahlin archives at Paradise Press[58] present a deliberate, consistent, and highly prolific collection of a true working craftsman. The partnership of two gentlemen from different worlds—who might not otherwise have interacted in the any other capacity—made the Aries Press a special, if not obscure, instance in the history of the private press.

Bibliography of the Aries Press

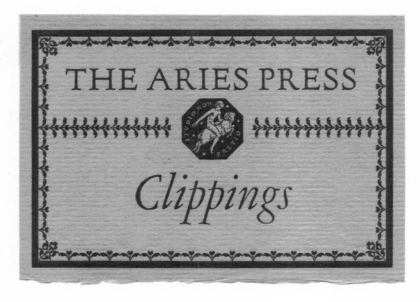

"Aries Press Specimens" and "Aries Press Clippings" labels.

1925

Books

1. *Niagara*. Evelyn M. Watson. Aries Book Club. 1925. 8 pp. 6" × 9"
   Type: Nicolas Cochin and Fournier le Jeune. 180 copies.

Booklets

2. *Aries* magazine. Volume 2, Number 1, Winter 1925.
   (Note: No known copies of Volume 1 have been found).

3. *In Memoriam*. Reginald Stanley Young. *The Argonne*, October
   Ninth MCMXVIII. Privately printed for friends of Liezet Young.
   9" × 13". Type: Hadriano. 100 copies.

4. *Nicolaus Jenson*. By Horatio F. Brown. Keepsake for the
   Aries Book Club. 4 pp. 7.5" × 10". Type: Italian Oldstyle.
   Binding: Folded sheet. 50 copies.
   Colophon: *Done for members of the Aries Book Club by Spencer
   Kellogg Jr. assisted by Emil Georg Sahlin, Compositor, with border
   design and initials by Harriet Blacking, at the Aries Press in the
   village of Eden, County of Erie, New York. Of this Keepsake, in the
   month of September, 1925, Fifty copies have been printed on Italian
   hand made paper, on the press used by William Morris for the
   Kelmscott Chaucer. The paragraph heading the sketch is from the
   dedication in Jenson's St. Thomas of Aquinas of 1480. The material
   used is from 'The Venetian Printing press' by Horatio F. Brown:
   John C. Nimmo, Publisher, London, 1891.*

ARIES

 BEING THE PRIVATE PRESS
OF SPENCER KELLOGG, JR

 Printed for the Principal and
Teachers of the Eden High
School on the occasion of their
visit to the Aries Press, which
is in the Village of Eden, County of Erie,
State of New York, on Friday May the
29th, A.D., 1925.

Done on Umbria Italian Hand-made
Paper, dampened before printing, and on
the hand press used by WILLIAM MORRIS
for many of his finest books, notably the
Kelmscott Chaucer, at 14 Upper Mall,
Hammersmith, England.

Of this keepsake twenty copies have
been printed of which this is No

Typography by AXEL EDWARD SAHLIN, *Composition by*
EMIL GEO. SAHLIN, *Presswork by* SPENCER KELLOGG, JR

Ephemera & Keepsakes

5. *Ballade*. François Villon. Keepsake for the Aries Book Club.
    4 pp. 6.5" × 9". Type: Garamond and Fournier le Jeune. Binding:
    Four-page French fold. 100 copies; 63 additional copies on
    handmade paper.
    Colophon: *Of this Keepsake done for members of the Aries Book
    Club, 63 copies have been printed on Italian handmade paper in
    the month of December 1925 at the Aries Press, Eden, New York.
    In addition for sale at the Aries Book Shop, 100 copies have been
    printed on ordinary paper. The Translation of the 'Ballade que feit
    Villion á la requeste de sa mere' has been taken from 'The Poems of
    François Villon' by H. De Vere Stacpoole, John Lane Co., Publishers,
    New York, MCMXIV.*

6. *Aries*. Broadside. *Printed for the Principal and Teachers of Eden
    High School on the occasion of their visit to the Aries Press.... May
    the 29th, A.D. 1925.* Edition of 20. Printed on the Kelmscott
    Albion press.

7. *Dreamland*. Rhyme sheet series #1. By Edgar Allan Poe. Illustrated
    by Elizabeth MacKinstry. 9.5" × 19.5". Type: Hadriano, 210 copies,
    (11 on Japan vellum signed by the artist and printer).

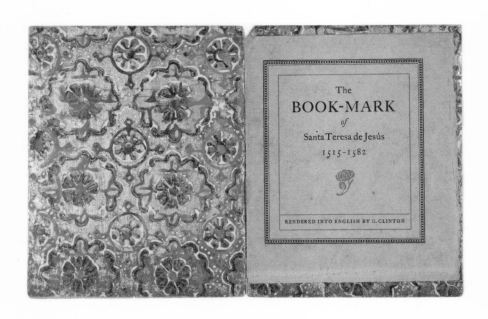

The
BOOK-MARK
of
Santa Teresa de Jesús
1515-1582

RENDERED INTO ENGLISH BY G. CLINTON

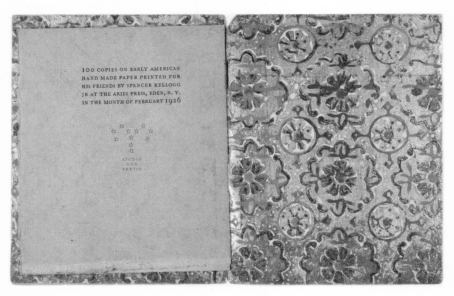

100 COPIES ON EARLY AMERICAN
HAND MADE PAPER PRINTED FOR
HIS FRIENDS BY SPENCER KELLOGG
JR AT THE ARIES PRESS, EDEN, N. Y.,
IN THE MONTH OF FEBRUARY 1926

STUDIO
NON
PRETIO

1926

Books

8. *The Ghost Ship*. By Robert Middleton. Preface by Arthur Machen.
    20 pp. 6" × 8.5". Type: English Caslon. Binding: Deep blue and gold
    marbled paper over boards with cloth back stamped in gold. 300
    copies.

Booklets

9. *The Book Mark of Santa Teresa de Jesus: 1515–1582.*
    From the Spanish by George Clinton Jr. 4 pp. 3.5" × 4.5".
    Type: Caslon. Binding: Chinese gold flowered paper covers.

10. *Ad Torquatum*. Q. Horti Flacci, Carm. IV. 7. Rendered into
    English by G. Clinton Jr., Latin and English. 4 pp. 6" × 9". Type:
    Garamont. Binding: Tile red (terracotta) paper covers. 100 copies.
    Colophon: *One hundred copies printed on Kelmscott Handmade
    paper by Spencer Kellogg Jr. at the Aries Press, village of Eden, New
    York March MCMXXVI.*

11. *The Aries Press: A Recapitulation of the First Year*. 8 pp. 5" × 8".
    Type: Goudy Modern, Forum. Binding: Blue wraps. 300 copies.
    Colophon: *Printed By Spencer Kellogg Junior To Commemorate The
    First Anniversary Of The Founding Of The Press.*

12. *The Aries Press* (Cover by James Guthrie). Spencer Kellogg Jr., 8
    pp. 5.5" × 7."
    Type: Goudy Modern. Self Covers. 300 copies.

Spencer Kellogg & Sons

Incorporated

*Vegetable Oil Producers
and Refiners*

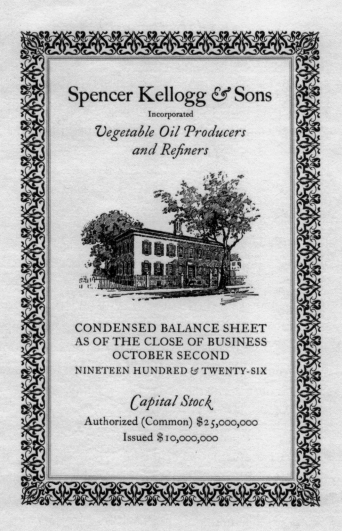

CONDENSED BALANCE SHEET
AS OF THE CLOSE OF BUSINESS
OCTOBER SECOND
NINETEEN HUNDRED & TWENTY-SIX

Capital Stock

Authorized (Common) $25,000,000
Issued $10,000,000

Keepsakes

13. "Dear Friend I beg you listen." Valentine. Printed for the friends of Lida and Spencer Kellogg, Jr. Cuts by Joseph Crawhall. 5.5" × 14". Printed on yellow paper. Edition of 150.

14. "Sweet Cider." Rhyme sheet. Series #2. By Spencer Kellogg, Jr. Illustrated by J.J. Lankes. 9.5" × 20.5". Type: Cloister Initials & Caslon. 210 copies.

15. "Sweet Cider." Rhyme sheet. Series #2. By Spencer Kellogg, Jr. Illustrated by J.J. Lankes (on Japan vellum). 9.5" × 20.5". Type: Cloister Initials & Caslon. 11 copies.

Ephemera

16. Aries Press order sheet. "Please enter my order for," 5" × 7". Type: Poliphilus and Blado. Pale orange paper.

17. *The Ghost Ship*. Prospectus. 4 pp. French fold. 5.5" × 8". Type: Caslon.

18. *The Ghost Ship*. Order acknowledgement. 4 pp. (inside blank). 4" × 5.5". Blue and black ink. Type: Caslon.

19. Aries Press announcement sheet. (For *Ad Torquatum* and *The Bookmark of Santa Maria de Jesus*. 4 pp. 4.5" × 7.5". Type: Caslon. Printed in red and black (typed inside: "Errata: For Santa Maria read Santa Teresa").

20. Spencer Kellogg & Sons corporate balance sheet. Type: Caslon. ☞ 1926.

A MAJESTIC OAK BROODS OVER
me. A smoldering sun is sinking as I dream.
The quiet of a late September afternoon, preg-
nant with deep meanings, is broken only by
the slow run of an occasional wavelet along the

21. *The Bells*. By Edgar Allan Poe. Christmas 1926 booklet. 4 pp.
    5" × 6". Type: Caslon. Red paper wraps.
    Colophon: *Typography, Woodcut and Printing by Emil Georg Sahlin
    at the Aries Press in the Village of Eden New York.*

1927

Books

22. *The Oak by the Waters of Rowan*. By Spencer Kellogg, Jr. Foreword
    by Evelyn M. Watson. Decorations by Wanda Gág.
    28 pp. 6" × 9". Type: Goudy "Antique", Baldo Italic, Greco
    Adronado. Binding: Blue and black leaf pattern over boards.
    295 copies.

Booklet

23. *Autumn Embers: A Poem*. By Spencer Kellogg, Jr., Decorations
    by Wanda Gág. 8 pp. 8.75" × 13". Type: Caslon Italic. Brown paper
    wraps, title in gold on front cover. 195 copies.

Ephemera

24. *The Oak by the Waters of Rowan*. Prospectus. 4 pp. 5.75" × 8". Type:
    Goudy "Antique", Baldo Italic, Greco Adronado.

25. *The Oak by the Waters of Rowan*. Subscription blank. 4" × 5". Type:
    Blado Italic. One color.

26. *Verses*. Trial title page settings (multiple variations). Trial pages are
    held at Paradise Press and Dennison Library.

✠ Christmas Mcmxxvii ✠

✠ ✠ Little Town of Bethlehem ✠ ✠

O LITTLE town of Bethlehem,
    How still we see thee lie!
Above thy deep and dreamless sleep
The silent stars go by;
Yet in thy dark streets shineth
The everlasting Light;
The hopes and fears of all the years
Are met in thee tonight.

F OR Christ is born of Mary,
    And gathered all above,
While mortals sleep, the angels keep
Their watch of wondering love.
O morning stars, together
Proclaim the holy birth,
And praises sing to God the King,
And peace to men on earth!

H OW silently, how silently,
    The wondrous gift is given!
So God imparts to human hearts
The blessings of his heaven.
No ear may hear his coming,
But in this world of sin,
Where meek souls will receive him still,
The dear Christ enters in.

O HOLY Child of Bethlehem!
    Descend to us, we pray;
Cast out our sin, and enter in,
Be born in us today.
We hear the Christmas angels
The great glad tidings tell;
O come to us, abide with us,
Our Lord Immanuel!

GREETINGS

Julia Catherine & Emil Georg Sahlin

27. Christmas card. Little Town of Bethlehem, "Greetings Julia
☞ Catherine and Emil Georg Sahlin". 8" × 14". 50 copies, Type:
Cloister Black.
Colophon: *Of this "Greeting" Fifty copies have been printed damp*
on early Italian handmade paper and hand-illuminated by Emil
Georg Sahlin, Typographer and Designer, at the Aries Press, in the
Village of Eden, N.Y. Verses by Phillips Brooks. MCMXXVII

28. Greetings. Aries Hill House Lida & Spencer Kellogg Jr.
(verse by Washington Irving) 5" × 11". Christmas MCMXXVII,
Type: Cloister Black and Caslon.

1928

Books

29. *Verses.* By Gertrude Kellogg Clark. 37 pp. 5.5" × 8". Type: Caslon &
Caslon Italic. Patterned paper over boards. 300 copies.
Colophon: *300 Copies have been printed at the Aries Press, in*
the Village of Eden, New York, by Spencer Kellogg Jr., Assisted
by Emil Georg Sahlin. And finished in the month of January
MCMXXVIII.

30. *Little Songs by the Way, Set Down in Words.* Lois Kellogg Roth.
Drawings by Elizabeth MacKinstry. 5" × 7.5". Floral patterned
paper wraps. 95 copies.
Colophon: *95 copies of this book made for his daughter on the*
occasion of her Birthday by Spencer Kellogg Jr., assisted by Emil
Georg Sahlin... Drawings by Elizabeth Mackinstry... All finished in
this month of March 1928.

THE ARIES BOOK SHOP no longer exists except in the memories of its patrons. For five years at a loss of over two thousand dollars each year this unusual shop was maintained for your pleasure and that of others. In order to devote all of my time to writing and to the Aries Press I have closed the book shop doors. May I not ask you as a one time sharer in the delights of our old shop to make our financial deficit somewhat lighter by promptly settling your account thus saving us further trouble in its collection?

The amount of your bill is

THE ARIES PRESS
Eden, New York.

31. *Little Songs by the Way, Set Down in Words.* Lois Kellogg Roth. *5" × 7.5". Maquette with hand rendered illustrations and limited trial typesetting along with hand lettered poems. Black and Red stencil patterned paper covers. One Copy.*

32. *In Praise of My Lady.* William Morris. Decorations by Elizabeth MacKinstry. 6 pp., 8.5" × 13". Type: Aries. Binding: Quarterbound deep green Morocco and green marbled paper. 31 copies.

Booklet
33. *Dialogue at Christmas: A Poem.* By John Drinkwater. Decorations by Wanda Gág. 8 pp. 5.5" × 8.5". Type: Caslon Italic. Binding: Green paper with gold flecks wraps, title in gold on front cover. 150 copies.

Undated Ephemera

34. Aries book shelf, October. Single sheet. 11.5" × 9". Deep orange paper.

35. Aries Book Shop closure and bill notice, October. 4 pp. 6" × 9". Pale blue paper.

36. Letterhead: The Studio Aries Hill. 5" × 7". Handmade blue paper. Type: Aries.

37. Letterhead: Spencer Kellogg, Jr., Aries Hill, Village of Eden New York. 5.5" × 8". Type: Caslon Italic. With leaf ornament.

38. Letterhead: Spencer Kellogg, Jr., Aries Press, Village of Eden, Erie County, New York. 7.5" × 10" Type: Caslon Italic. With star ornament arrangement and "Studio Non Pretio."

39. Billhead: Spencer Kellogg, Jr., The Aries Press, Village of Eden, New York. Limited Edition. 6.75" × 7". Type: Caslon. With Aries "Studio Non Pretio" logo.

40. Note/Bookmark: "...We hope the inclosed [[sic]] folder..." Red ink. 2.5" × 6." Type: Poliphilus and Blado.

41. Envelope: Spencer Kellogg, Jr., Aries Press, Village of Eden, Erie County, New York. 4.5" × 6". Type: Blado.

42. Label: "Aries Press Clippings." 3.5" × 4.5". Type: Forum. Brown on yellow paper. One known copy.

43. Label: "Aries Press Specimens." 3.5" × 4.5". Type: Forum and Garamond Italic. Brown on yellow paper. One known copy.

44. Business card: EmilGeoSahlin, Eden, New York. Aries zodiac ☜ symbol inside mortise cut of printer.

Collections

Unique collections used as primary sources:

Buffalo & Erie Library Rare Book Room, Buffalo, NY
Collection of the author
Ella Strong Denison Library, Scripps College, Claremont, CA
The Grolier Club Library, New York City, NY
Melbert B. Cary, Jr. Graphic Arts Collection, Rochester Institute
    of Technology, Rochester, NY
The Newberry Library, Chicago, IL
Paradise Press Archives, Buffalo, NY
Syracuse University Special Collections, Syracuse, NY

Acknowledgments

Bruce Austin
Buffalo and Erie County Historical Society
Buffalo and Erie County Public Library
Timothy Conroy
Molly Cort
Eden Historical Society
Eric Jackson Forsberg
Grolier Club Library
Kathleen Heyworth
Amelia Hugill-Fontanel
Hal Leader
William Loos
Joseph Murray
David Pankow
Amy Pickard
Paul Romaine
Robert Rust
Judy Harvey Sahak
Marnie Soom
Ann Stevens
Jean-François Vilain

Notes

1. Emery Walker's talk on letterpress printing and illustration delivered to the Arts and Crafts Society, 15 November 1888. William S. Peterson, *The Kelmscott Press: A History of William Morris's Typographical Adventure* (Oakland, CA: University of California Press, 1991).

2. The partnership was infamous due to an acrimonious split in which Cobden-Sanderson destroyed the matrices and type of the Doves Press by dumping them into the Thames River.

3. http://mitpress.mit.edu/books/buffalo-architecture.

4. "A History of the City of Buffalo: Its Men and Institutions: Biographical Sketches of Leading Citizens," *Buffalo Evening News*, 1908, p. 110.

5. Anthony Bannon, *The Photo-Pictorialists of Buffalo* (Buffalo, NY: Media Study, 1981), p. 92.

6. Spencer Kellogg, "Buffalonian Paints Pictures in Paris," *Courier Express*, April 2, 1933, Sec 9, p. 1.

7. Elbert Hubbard was an executive at the Larkin Soap Company before leaving to start the Roycroft Campus. Hubbard was Darwin D. Martin's friend and mentor years before Martin enlisted Frank Lloyd Wright to design several significant buildings in Buffalo, NY. Curiously, Frank Lloyd Wright adopted his trademark hat, silk bow tie, and longish hair from Elbert Hubbard. See Meryle Secrest, *Frank Lloyd Wright: A Biography* (Chicago: University of Chicago Press, 1998), p. 158.

8. Darwin D. Martin to Frank Lloyd Wright, 21 April 1919, Frank Lloyd Wright Collections, The Design Archive at the University at Buffalo.

9. Darwin D. Martin to Frank Lloyd Wright, 28 August 1922, Frank Lloyd Wright Collections, The Design Archive at the University of Buffalo.

10. "It never made a penny, but he had a grand time with it" Spencer Kellogg, "Buffalonian Paints Pictures in Paris." *Courier Express*, April 2, 1933 Sec 9, p. 1.

11. Gomme, Laurence J., "The Little Book-Shop Around the Corner," from *The Colophon. New Series—A Quarterly for Bookmen* 2, no. 4 (New York: Pynson Printers Inc., Autumn 1937), p. 576.

12. *Aries Magazine* 2, no. 1, Winter 1925.

13. "Unique Haven for Bookworm," *Buffalo Commercial Advertiser and Journal* August 20, 1921.

14. Typed compilation of excerpts from notes from various customers and peers to the Aries Press, no date, Ella Strong Denison Library, Scripps College, Claremont, CA.

15. W. A. Dwiggins, "D.B. Updike and the Merrymount Press," *Fleuron*, no. 3 (London, UK: W. A. Dwiggins, 1924, pp 1–8.

16. *Aries* magazine 2, no. 1, Winter 1925, pp. 24–25

17. Gertrude Kellogg's *Verses*, from Grabau Press, 1921. It would be reprinted by Aries Press and become the second Aries title to receive one of the "50 Books" honors from the AIGA.

18. Credited only as Mrs. Sears and Miss Frederick.

19. *Specimen Book & Catalogue* (Jersey City, NJ: American Type Founders Company, 1923), pp. 282–83.

20. No documentation has been found on the actual production designers of the ATF books, however it was verbally conveyed to Harold Leader by his mentor, Emil Sahlin, that he and his brother worked on the epic 1923 ATF catalog.

21. Artists such as Claes Oldenburg, Jackson Pollock, and Sam Francis were given their first exposure to the art world through Martha Jackson. She often cited her Uncle Spencer for being an inspiration in her artistic pursuits.

22. May Morris, in Dard Hunter, *My Life with Paper* (New York: Knopf, 1958), p.36.

23. Clark, Gertrude Kellogg, *Verses* (Buffalo, NY: Gay Press, 1922), bound by John Grabau Art Bookbinding Studio, Buffalo, NY [31] leaves; 19 cm.

24. Spencer Kellogg, "Buffalonian Paints Pictures in Paris," *Courier Express*, April 2, 1933.

25. Emil Georg Sahlin interview with Hal Leader, *Printer*, Paradise Press.

26. The "Lost Goudy Types" are referred to as such because the drawings, patterns, and matrices for these typefaces were destroyed in a fire at Goudy's Village Press on January 26, 1939.

27. Frederic Goudy, *A Half-Century of Type Design and Typography* (New York: Typophiles, 1946), p. 145.

28. Daniel Berkeley Updike, *Printing Types, Their History, Forms, and Use* (Oxford University Press, 1922 (second printing of third edition) Vol. 1, pp. 71–72.

29. Frederic Goudy, *A Half-Century of Type Design and Typography* (New York: Typophiles, 1946) pp. 191-92.

30. Melbert B. Cary, Jr., *A Bibliography of the Village Press, 1903-1938* (New York: Press of the Woolly Whale, 1938), item 202, pp.175–76.

31. Frederic Goudy, *A Half-Century of Type Design and Typography* (New York: Typophiles, 1946), p. 143.

32. Ibid. p. 191.

33. This press was acquired from John DePol by the Melbert B. Cary, Jr. Collection at the Rochester Institute of Technology.

34. William Morris, *Some Thoughts on the Ornamented Mss. of the Middle Ages*, New York: Press of the Woolly Whale, 1934, essay by Melbert B. Cary Jr. "A Brief Account of the Wanderings of Albion Press No. 6551, Its Various Owners and the work it has done," p. 20.

35. "The Liberty Bell on the Kelmscott Goudy Press," *The Black Art* 1, no 2 (Summer 1962), p. 42.

36. Notes to the Aries Press, circa 1925–1928. Undated letter from Bruce Rogers. Perkins Autograph Letter Collection, Ella Strong Denison Library, Scripps College, Claremont, CA.

37. Letters found in the Perkins Autograph Letter Collection, Ella Strong Denison Library, Scripps College, Claremont, CA, http://ccdl.libraries.claremont.edu/cdm/landingpage/collection/pal.

38. Later in the mid-20th century a more prolific Aries Press emerged in Chicago, which published astrological and occult books.

39. Lois Kellogg, *Opposites* (Portland, Maine: The Mosher Press, 1933).

40. Unidentified author, "Spencer Kellogg, Buffalonian Paints Pictures in Paris," *Courier Express*, April 2, 1933.

41. Ibid.

42. "Spencer Kellogg Jr. is Dead at Age of 68 in California Home." *Buffalo Evening News*, December 20, 1944.

43. Correspondence to Miss Drake at Scripps College circa 1941.

44. Aries Press Sunrise Layouts, Specimen Case 2, Dr.1 Env 3-5. Perkins Autograph Letter Collection, Ella Strong Denison Library, Scripps College, Claremont, CA.

45. Letter from Spencer Kellogg to Miss Drake dated Sept. 13, 1941. Perkins Autograph Letter Collection, Ella Strong Denison Library, Scripps College, Claremont, CA.

46. This quote is compiled from hand-written and typed drafts of notes for Emil Sahlin lectures given to schools and printers' groups. These were hand-written and typed notes that were almost the same, but the author referred to the typed version to make sure of certain words that were hard to read. The hand-written account was longer and had more information.

47. Draft of notes for Emil Sahlin lectures given to schools and printers' groups. Collection of the Paradise Press, Buffalo, NY.

48. Letter to unknown recipient from Emil Sahlin, undated, collection of the author.

49. Ibid.

50. Letters from Spencer Kellogg to J.J. Lankes, 1925–1928, Lankes Collection, Buffalo and Erie County Public Library, Buffalo, NY.

51. Letter from Spencer Kellogg, Jr. to Wilbur Macy Stone, December 3, 1926, Aries Press collection, Buffalo and Erie County Public Library, Buffalo, NY.

52. Wilbur Macy Stone to Spencer Kellogg, Jr., August 15, 1930, Aries Press collection, Buffalo and Erie County Public Library, Buffalo, NY.

53. Spencer Kellogg to Wilbur Macy Stone, September 7, 1930, Aries Press collection, Buffalo and Erie County Public Library, Buffalo, NY.

54. *The Liberty Bell on the Kelmscott Goudy Press*, Yellow Barn Press, 1996, pp. 1–6

55. Spencer Kellogg, Jr., *Out of the Deep* (Santa Barbara, CA: Schauer Printing Studio, 1944), 68 pp., hard cover. One of 250 copies.

56. Aurora Historical Society Tape #106. Emil Georg Sahlin, interview by Ken Whitney,transcribed by Christine Kroschel, September 23, 1979, in *Talk Less, Listen More, Visiting with Aurora's Elders*, 2003,

57. Specimen Case 2, Dr. 1, Env. 3 & 5—'Sunrise' Layouts (Marsh Poems) Perkins Autograph Letter Collection, Ella Strong Denison Library, Scripps College, Claremont, CA.

58. Collection of the Paradise Press, Buffalo, NY.

Index

Note: Page numbers in *italics* indicate illustrations.

About the Author

Richard Kegler is the Director of the Wells College Book Arts Center in Aurora, New York. He founded both the P22 Type Foundry and the Western New York Book Arts Center in Buffalo, New York. Kegler is a letterpress printer and book designer with a long-standing interest in printing history.

Colophon

Type
Kennerley Pro by Lanston Type Company,
based on Kennerley Old Style by Frederic Goudy, 1911

Paper
Mohawk Via 70# Laid Natural White

Printing and binding
Global Printing, Alexandria, Virginia

This book was made possible, in part,
through the generosity of Global Printing
and, in part, by support from
John C. Williams